IN THE NEWS

DL 130   **GRADES 4-6**

A Unit for Investigating Newspapers

Written by Katherine Howe and Judith Edelstein   Illustrated by Mary Lou Johnson

Students discover business, editori advertising, sports, humor

DAILY PRESS

ISBN 1-883055-38-5

Edited by Dianne Draze and Sonsie Conroy

About Copyrights and Reproduction

Contents

Information for the Instructor

People want to know what is going on in their world. They want to know what their neighbors and elected officials are doing, what the weather will be like, where they can find a special sale, and what types of entertainment are available. All this information (and more) is available in a newspaper.

Newspapers first appeared over 2,000 years ago, filling the need for people to be informed about what was happening in their environment. During these 2,000 years, newspapers have taken on different looks and functions. Today one can find newspapers with a wide, general appeal, but also a great number of newspapers with a small focus and readership. Since the advent of radio, television and the Internet, newspapers have experienced declining readership, but they still remain an important source of current, concise information.

This unit is designed to introduce students to the many forms of information and opinions they will find in their local and regional newspapers. After an introduction to newspapers in general, they will delve into each section of the newspaper to discover all the many facets of this important form of communication.

As a result of completing the activities in this book, students will:

- become familiar with newspaper terminology
- analyze the format and structure of a newspaper
- compare different types of newspapers, their goals and readership
- compare styles of writing in different sections of a newspaper
- demonstrate an understanding of newspaper writing styles by writing their own articles
- compare the newspaper to other reporting media and other forms of communication
- analyze the kinds of information that can be found in different sections of the newspaper
- create an original newspaper
- determine the usefulness of advertising in the newspaper

This book provides an easy-to-use format that incorporates several different ways to present information. **Lesson plans** provide step-by-step instructions for group lessons. Each lesson also has a list of suggested **extensions** for projects that will give students opportunities to present information about newspapers in creative ways. **Worksheets** are reproducible pages that present information about different aspects of newspapers and either provide ways to apply the knowledge or guidelines for projects. They are intended to be a resource for review and application. They can be used to supplement a group lesson, you can do the group lessons without the worksheets, or you can use the worksheets exclusively as projects for independent study. As a whole, this unit is a complete guide for introducing students to all the most important concepts involved in newspapers.

Group Lessons

Lesson 1 - A Means of Communication

Objective
Students will evaluate the function of a newspaper as a means of communication.

Materials
newspapers, worksheet entitled "History of Newspapers," page 19

Procedure
1. As a group, list all the different ways people can communicate an idea to other people.
2. List the attributes of these vehicles of communication — speed, reliability, able to reach a large number of people, entertaining, etc.
3. Pass out copies of newspaper for students to look through. Mark the attributes from step two that apply to a newspaper.
4. Discuss how newspapers compare to other means of communication.
5. Discuss whether students think that newspapers will be replaced by television or electronic newspapers on the Internet. What might be the advantages and disadvantages of a newspaper compared to these other ways to get information?

Extension
Essay - Have students write essays on one of the following themes:
Newspapers: An Endangered Species
Newspapers: A Vehicle of Communication
Newspapers: A Creative Medium

Researching and Recreating History - Read and discuss the worksheet entitled "History of Newspapers." Also research newspaper articles that appeared in your community newspaper in years past. What kinds of events were in the news 50 years ago? 100 years ago? Using archival records of newspapers and records of historic events in your community, have students create a newspaper that might have been published 100 years ago.

Lesson 2 - The News Article

Objective
Students will be able to demonstrate their understanding of newspaper writing and important elements of any news article by writing an original article.

Materials
front pages of newspapers, paper, pencils, worksheets entitled:
"The News Story," page 20
"Types of News Articles," page 21
"Eyewitness News Story," page 22

Procedure
1. Discuss the following information with students:
   - There are different kinds of articles in a newspaper. A straight news story reports recent news in a concise format. Most writing in newspapers is informational.
   - These newspaper articles answer six questions — who, what, when, where, why and how, known as 5 W + H.
   - The answer to "what" appears in the first part of straight news stories more consistently than the other elements.
   - An article is composed of a headline, a lead, and a summary.
   - The headline briefly describes the main point of the story. It is designed to catch the reader's attention.
   - The lead is the opening section of the news story. It is a brief statement of the story's essential fact(s) or theme. By reading the first paragraph (sometimes sentence) in a news article, the reader should have a good idea of what the story is about. The first sentence does not answer all the questions, but it covers the most essential points.
   - The summary is an elaboration on the lead. Here the reporter fills in additional information about the story. The most important facts are presented first and the less important facts follow.

- Most newspaper writing (except on the editorial page) does not express opinions. It is designed to give people the basic facts and then elaborate on those facts with details and quotations.
- Newspaper writing is not as descriptive as fictional writing.
- Newspaper articles must be:
  1. accurate
  2. balanced - present both sides of an issue and complete facts
  3. objective - show no personal bias
  4. clear and concise
  5. recent
- There are several different types of news articles. They are:

  straight news - news that is reported in a conventional, straightforward manner for informational purposes

  feature - stories that are written to entertain or supplement the regular news, providing more in-depth or personal coverage

  editorial - expresses the opinion of the editor or publisher of the paper

  eyewitness - offers a first-hand perspective on an event

  investigative - in-depth report on a topic that has significant bearing on public affairs, usually aimed at uncovering wrongdoings.

2. As a group, analyze the front page of the newspaper. Discuss what is different about the front page from the rest of the paper. What kind of news makes it to the front page?

3. Choose several articles from the front page and discuss the following:
   - What kind of information can be found in the headlines?
   - What do you know about the article from reading the first sentence? the first paragraph?
   - Can you find the answer to the questions, who, what, where, when, why and how?

4. Give students an article from your local newspaper and have them underline the lead and the sentences that answer the questions who, what, where, when, why and how.

5. Ask students to respond to the following situation.

   Extra, Extra! You're a front page headline. What do you say? Tell us what is happening by answering the questions who, what, where, when, why and how.

   Have them create headlines and write news articles for these headlines by filling in the facts for who, what, where, when, why and how and writing the articles following the guidelines discussed earlier. Their articles can be fictional or about real situations.

Extensions

Pictures - Have students draw pictures to accompany their news stories.

Different News Articles - Have students go through the worksheet entitled "Types of News Articles" that introduces different types of news articles in addition to straight stories.

Eyewitness Stories - Eyewitness stories are enjoyable for students to write because they can be more creative that writing straight news. Use the worksheet entitled "Eyewitness News Story" to have students write a news article about an event they have personally experienced.

Lesson 3 - Objectivity

Objective
Students will show an understanding of a newspaper's role in shaping attitudes, ideas and opinions by identifying and rewriting biased material.

Materials
newspapers

Procedure
1. Give students the following headlines and ask them to discuss the different ideas these would create in the minds of the newspaper's readership.
   - *Mob Riot Brings the City to a Standstill*
   - *Demonstrators Stop Traffic at Four Intersections*

- *Nation Sees an Alarming Rise in Teenage Smoking*
- *Nation's Leaders Propose Ways to Deal with Teenage Smoking*
- *Goldilocks - Lost in the Woods - Saved by Bears*
- *Goldilocks - Breaking and Entering Charges Dropped*
- *Tigers Advance to League Finals*
- *Tigers Will Meet a Challenge at League Finals*
- *Scientists Find a Way to Predict Earthquakes*
- *Earthquake - Is the Big Killer Coming?*

2. Discuss the fact that one of the outstanding goals of newspaper reporting is that it be objective. Reporters try to present the facts of a story in a fair, impartial manner. Historically newspapers have not always tried to be objective. Frequently, newspaper have been blatant about their efforts to report news in such a way that it would turn public opinion in one direction or another. While the aim is to be fair and unbiased, papers sometimes present information in such a way as to favor one perspective or imply that something is better or worse than what actually happened. The choice of words for headlines, the way articles are written, sources that are quoted, and opinions expressed in the editorial section often show a certain bias and influence the attitudes of people who read the paper.

3. Have students find articles or headlines that show a bias. Discuss the bias presented.

4. Have students rewrite the following headlines to be more objective:

- *Goldilocks Caught Red Handed*
- *Man with Flute Kidnaps All of Town's Children*
- *Wolf Terrorizes Pig Compound*
- *Woodsman Puts an End to Evil Wolf's Reign of Terror*
- *Foolish Boy Gives Away Cow in Exchange for a Handful of Worthless Beans*

Lesson 4 - Photography

Objective
Students will be able to identify the function of photographs in a newspaper and determine what makes a good news photograph.

Materials
newspapers, worksheet entitled "News Photography," page 23

Procedure
1. Choose a page from your newspaper that has one or two photographs but no advertising that includes photographs or illustrations. Ask students to turn to this page in their copies of the newspaper.

2. Ask students, "Where were your eyes drawn to first? Why?"

3. Have students look through the paper for other pages with photographs. Then have them in pairs complete the statement, "The purpose of photographs in the newspaper is to . . ." Share the answers.

4. Have students look through the paper and then discuss:

- What are the best photographs you found?
- Why are they good?
- What do they add to the articles?
- Is there information in the photographs that cannot be told by words alone?

5. Have students do the worksheet entitled "News Photography."

Extensions
Pictures - In preparation for making a class newspaper at the end of this unit, have students get cameras and begin taking pictures of events or situations that could be used in the newspaper that they will produce. Use black and white film.

Photojournalism - Photojournalism is different from the single photos that accompany a news article. Photojournalism is a news report in which the story is told by a series of pictures. There is usually copy or captions that explain the photos, but the page or article is predominately photographs. These photographic essays are usually found in magazines, but you sometimes find them in newspapers. Have students use photojournalism to explain the step-by-step procedure to do something or to report on a happening at your school.

Lesson 5 - Parts of a Newspaper

Objective
Students will be able to distinguish different sections of a newspaper and identify the type of news that one would find in a particular section.

Materials
newspapers, worksheets entitled:
"Parts of a Newspaper," page 24
"News Coverage," page 25

Procedure
1. Give students copies of newspapers to review either individually or in small groups. Have students list the sections of the newspaper and briefly describe the types of articles that are included in each section.

2. Discuss the location of world news, local news, want ads, business news, sports news, and editorials.

3. Analyze the different techniques the newspaper uses to call attention to articles or pieces of information — things like different type faces and sizes of type for headlines and subheads, pictures, and inset copy. Discuss which sections seem to have the most pictures. Point out that the front page and editorial page do not have advertising, but most other sections of the paper do contain ads. Discuss other differences students notice about the various sections of the paper.

4. Have students complete the worksheet entitled "What is a Newspaper?"

Extensions
Comparison - Have students select two different sections on the newspaper and compare them in a Venn diagram, listing things that are characteristic of each section and also common characteristics.

Calculations - Using the worksheet entitled "News Coverage," have students calculate the amount of space that is devoted to different types of articles.

Personal Preference - Have students tell (orally or in writing) for which section of the newspaper they would want to write and explain why.

Lesson 6 - Local News

Objective
Students will be able to distinguish local news from other news coverage and be able to identify the types of local issues that are covered in news stories.

Materials
newspapers, worksheet entitled "Local News," page 26

Procedure
1. Divide students into groups of two or three and have them look for local news in their papers.

2. Have them answer the question, "What kinds of events are reported in this paper?" Then have them categorize the topics. Ask them, "Which categories have the most articles? Why? Is this what most people are interested in reading about?"

3. Have students write a news article about a local event using the worksheet entitled "Local News."

Extensions
Survey - Using the categories of news topics from your class discussion, have students survey their friends and family to find out what kind of local news people most like to read. Compile individual results to make a class graph.

Comparison - Compare different media (radio, television, newspaper, and Internet) to find out where you can find the most up-to-date, complete coverage of local news.

Lesson 7 - National and World News

Objective
Students will be able to distinguish world and national news from other news coverage and be able to identify the types of local issues that are covered in news stories.

Materials
newspapers, worksheets entitled:
"World and National News," page 27
"News Services," page 28

Procedure
1. Define national and world news. National news is news that involves people beyond your immediate community. It could, of course, take place in your town or state and still have a national impact. World news is news that takes place in other countries or involves other countries of the world. Discuss the fact that while most newspapers have a special section for state, national and world news, these articles may appear in other areas, especially on the front page.

2. Divide students into pairs and ask them to look through their newspapers and find examples of local, state, national and world news stories.

3. Give students the following headlines and ask them to indicate if they are local, state, national, or world news.
   - Leaders of Three Nations Meet for Pollution Conference (world)
   - Service Station Owner Fined for Pollution (local)
   - State Legislature Enacts Tougher Pollution Rules (state)
   - South American Nations Unite to Save the Rain Forest (world)
   - Fire Breaks Out in Downtown Restaurant (local)
   - Pests Threaten State's Agriculture (state)
   - Archaeologists Discover Ancient Buried City (world)
   - Supreme Court Reverses Lower Court's Decision (national)
   - Airlines Announce Rate Hikes for International Flights (world/national)
   - Middle East Summit Date Set (world)
   - Computer Bug Wipes Out Computers Around the Globe (world)
   - New Governor's Mansion Costs Taxpayers Plenty (state)
   - President Announces New Funds for School Computers (national)

4. As a group, have students look through the newspaper and make a list of headlines for world news and note where the story originates. Keep this list and add to it for several days. What cities are in the news? Why? In which countries/continents are these cities located?

5. Have students do the worksheet entitled "World News."

Extension
Bulletin Board - As a group, find at least one news story for each continent. Create a bulletin board using these articles. Ask students to review the articles. Based on the articles, what generalizations can they make about each continent and what is happening there?

News Services - Discuss the fact that most world news comes from news agencies. These are agencies that have reporters stationed in foreign countries. They provide news stories and photographs to papers that subscribe to the service. Have students complete the exercise on the worksheet entitled "News Services."

Lesson 8 - The Editorial Page

Objective
Students will be able to distinguish the types of articles that appear in the editorial section of the newspaper and will analyze one article.

Materials
newspapers, worksheets entitled:
"Opinion Page," page 29
"Letters to the Editor," page 30
"Political Cartoons," page 31

Procedure

1. Explain that the editorial page is one place where the writers do not have to be totally unbiased. Articles and letters on this page express the opinion of the writer.

2. Have students look through the editorial page of the newspaper and discuss the following:

   - What kinds of articles are on the editorial page? (editor's opinion, articles by columnists that express opinions, editorial cartoons, letters to the editor)
   - What kind of opinions are expressed and what kind of issues are discussed?
   - Find one article with which you agree.
   - Find one article with which you disagree.
   - What is the editorial cartoon suggesting?

3. Have students do the worksheet entitled "Opinion Page."

Extensions

Political Cartoons - Have students do the worksheet entitled "Political Cartoons." Then have them collect five cartoons, mount each one on a piece of paper and explain the cartoonist's message. They should be able to explain how the caption and the picture work together to give the reader information or an opinion on this issue.

Editorializing - Have students create their own editorials. They should choose an important problem in their school or community to discuss. In the editorials, they should explain the problem, state their positions on this issue, and give reasons for feeling this way. They should try to be as persuasive as possible.

Comparison - Have students compare the editorial pages from at least two different newspapers and write a paper or give an oral report that discusses how the articles are similar or different. Have them discuss which paper is easiest to understand and with which paper they agree.

Letters to the Editor - Have students read five letters to the editor and explain why each person was writing and what his or her feelings are. Then have each student choose one of the letters to which he or she will respond. Use the "Letters to the Editor" worksheet for the response letters.

Lesson 9 - Humor in the Newspaper

Objective
Students will discover and analyze the different ways newspapers use humor.

Materials
comic section of the newspaper, worksheets entitled:
"Humor in the Newspaper," page 32
"The Comics," page 33

Procedure
1. Ask students:

   - What is your favorite part of the newspaper? (Most students will answer the comics.)
   - Why is this your favorite?
   - What make the comics so appealing?

2. Review the following information:
   - Satirical cartoons in newspapers originated in the eighteenth century.
   - Comics developed in America in the twentieth century as a device to increase newspaper circulation.
   - *The Yellow Kid,* which originated in 1895, was one of the first popular comics.
   - *The Katzenjammer Kids* originated in 1897 and was also an early comic favorite.
   - Several cartoons, like *Peanuts,* have experienced long-running success.
   - Comics cover a wide range of topics, including humor, adventure, science fiction, and crime.
   - Many cartoon strips or characters have been the basis for successful movies and television specials.

3. Discuss where else in a newspaper you can find humor. Include humorous stories, photographs, essays by humorous columnists. Find examples of these humorous additions to the newspaper.

4. Have students do the worksheets entitled "Humor in the Newspaper" and "The Comics."

Extensions
Creating Humor - Give students copies of cartoons without the captions and let them write their own dialogue.

Bulletin Board - Create a bulletin board with the title *Humor in the Newspaper*. Have students collect their favorite stories, cartoons and commentaries to put on the board.

Movie Proposal - Have students choose a comic strip and propose a movie or television special based on this comic or one of the characters. They should make oral presentations as if they were trying to persuade a producer to make the movie.

What If? - Have students choose two comic characters, one from one comic strip and one from a different strip. Then have them create a cartoon in which the characters meet and interact.

Lesson 10 - Other Sections of the Newspaper

Objective
Students will analyze several other sections of the newspaper to find distinguishing characteristics.

Materials
newspapers, worksheets entitled:
"Business News," page 34
"Sports," page 35
"Humorous Sports," page 36
"Entertainment," page 37
"Travel Information," page 38
"Weather," page 39

Note
Once you have covered the main sections in the newspaper, there will still be many other interesting sections to study. If not on a daily basis, most newspapers contain at least weekly sections for sports, health, science, home and garden, business, technology, gossip columns, advice columns, travel, and weather.

At this point, you may want to assess how much time you want to devote to studying each section in depth. We have provided worksheets to introduce students to several different sections in the newspaper. You may wish to use the worksheets provided to have each student analyze several of these sections. You may also choose to divide students into groups, having each group select a section of the paper and report back to the whole class.

The procedure that follows is a generalized lesson plan for studying any of these additional sections of the newspaper. You can adapt it to fit any of the sections to which you wish to introduce students. You can cover several or all of the news sections depending on your instructional goals and time constraints.

Procedure
1. Have students turn to the chosen section of the newspaper. Ask them:
   - What kinds of information do you find here?
   - Who might be interested in this news?
   - Why would you consult this section?
   - Are the articles straight news, feature stories, commentaries, advice, syndicated, or some combination of these types of stories?
   - How do you read sports statistics? stock prices? weather information? movie ratings? birth announcements?
   - What advice is given in this column/section? Is this useful advice? Who might need this information? Do you agree?

2. Have students do one of the following things with the information in the section they are studying:
   - Identify the most interesting (important, useful) information.
   - Point out how the writers get your attention. How is this like/unlike other sections of the paper?
   - Choose an article and give your opinion about it.
   - Put the information in another form, like a graph or diagram.
   - Compare the same section in two different papers.

- Summarize the information. Then tell how it applies to your life.
- Determine how this information will affect your life/the lives of people in your community.
- How might someone from another country/another time in history view this?
- Make a list of questions this raises.

Lesson 11 - Audience and Speciality Newspapers

Objective
Students will compare the designs of various newspapers to see how each meets the needs of its readers.

Materials
various newspapers, especially some newspapers that cater to a particular group of readers like *The Wall Street Journal, The Christian Science Monitor*, papers from the local high school, as well as several local and metropolitan papers

Procedure
1. Discuss how newspapers cater to specific audiences. These audiences have different characteristics and interests. Mass appeal newspapers cater to the interests of the mass audience with lots of photographs, a wide variety of information and articles that are quick to read. Many papers, however, are written for a smaller, more focused readership. Their articles, the amount of space they devote to different sections, and their editorial content will be influenced by the people who subscribe to the paper.
2. Pass out papers and let students look through the variety of newspapers.
3. Divide students into groups of four and select a recorder for each group. Ask the recorder to write down the ideas for the group as they discuss the following points.
   - What kind of reader is each newspaper written for?
   - How do you know this?
   - What are some of the needs of the readers of each paper?
   - Does the newspaper meet these needs?

- What improvements could be made to the newspaper that would enable it to better meet the needs of the readers or make it more attractive to the readers?

3. Ask students to start thinking about the kind of newspaper they like to create. What focus will the paper have (for example, fashion, sports, school activities)? Who will read the paper? What are the needs of these readers?

Lesson 12 - Advertising

Objective
Students will study several forms of advertising in newspapers and be able to determine the usefulness of advertising in newspapers.

Materials
newspapers, worksheets entitled:
"Advertising," page 40
"Classified Advertisements," page 41
"Using Newspaper Advertising," page 42

Procedure
1. Discuss the following:
   - Advertisers pay money to run their ads in the newspaper.
   - Most newspapers contain about 60% advertising and 40% news and commentary.
   - Advertisers will usually choose to run their advertisements in sections of the paper that are read by people who are most interested in their products. Therefore, a company selling patio furniture might want to advertise in the home and garden section, while a sports equipment store would probably choose the sports section.
2. Cut out advertisements from several sections of the newspaper that represent a variety of products and services. Show students the ads and ask them to identify the section(s) of the newspaper where these ads might be found.
3. Give students several products or services and ask them to pretend that they are trying to reach potential customers and to identify in which section of the newspaper they would choose to advertise.

4. Have students do the worksheet entitled "Advertising."

5. Look at the classified advertising section. Have students find one thing that they would like to buy and one job they would find interesting.

6. Have students complete the worksheet entitled "Classified Advertisements."

Extension
Evaluation - Discuss, "Are advertisements in newspapers a good thing or a bad thing?"

Application - Have students use the worksheet entitled "Using Newspaper Advertising" to create a shopping list for an outing.

Lesson 13 - Field Trip

Objective
Students will observe the everyday work conditions of a real newspaper.

Materials
transportation

Procedure
1. Arrange for a trip to the local newspaper or have a guest speaker from the newspaper come to your classroom.

2. Have students prepare questions that they would like to have answered prior to the trip or presentation.

3. After the trip or presentation review what students learned, what they found most interesting, and what job they found most intriguing.

Extension
Diagram - Have students make a diagram showing the steps a newspaper goes through to get a news event in the paper, showing the roles of the reporters, editors and photographers.

Help Wanted Ad - Have students write a help wanted ad for a position at the newspaper.

Lesson 14 - Making a Newspaper

Objective
Students will demonstrate knowledge of newspaper format and content by creating an original newspaper.

Materials
paper, writing materials, computers or typewriters

Procedure
1. Divide the class into groups.

2. Have each group decide on a focus and discuss the organization of their newspapers. They should discuss:
   - job assignments
   - focus of the newspaper
   - type of reader
   - format, size, sections
   - advertising
   - photographs

3. Give each group a week or two to conduct interviews, gather information and write articles for their newspapers. The final products should be papers that reflect a specific focus and include several of the components of an actual newspaper.

Lesson 15 - Newspaper Analogies and Comparisons

Objective
Students will be able to form an analogy between themselves and different features of a newspaper.

Materials
none

Procedure
1. Seat students in a circle so everyone has eye contact with the rest of the group. Ask them to respond to the following imaginary situation:
   - Imagine you are a section of the newspaper. What are you? Why?
   - What would be the most prominent headline on your first page?
   - What photographs would be on your first page?

- What kind of people would read your articles?
- What would you like to say to these people?

2. As a group list some other forms of creative expression such as poetry, novels, films, videos, musical arrangements, computer programs, speeches, sculptures, and painting. Compare newspapers to these other forms of expression and communication by discussing the following points:
   - How is a newspaper like or unlike these other forms of expression?
   - Is a newspaper able to be completely free and creative? Why?
   - What guidelines might apply to newspapers that do not apply to other forms of expression?
   - How does a newspaper use literary devices like metaphor, simile or alliteration?

Supplementary and Culminating Activities

Panel Discussion - Divide students into several groups of four. Have each group choose one of the following topics and have a panel discussion with each person contributing ideas.
- What things would be different if newspapers had never existed?
- What are the effects of yellow journalism?
- What changes are in store for newspapers in the future?
- What is the relationship between newspapers and freedom?
- What is the relationship between newspapers and politics?

Famous People - Use the worksheet entitled "Newspaper People" on page 43 to acquaint students with people who have been most influential in the newspaper business. In addition to looking up these men and matching each one with his accomplishments, have them choose one person for an in-depth report.

Future of Newspapers - Discuss the changes that have taken place in newspaper publishing since the advent of radio, television and the Internet. Then have students use the worksheet entitled "News in the Future" to write a fitting epitaph for newspapers.

Debate - Using the topics suggested on page 45, have students stage a debate, with one team choosing the proposition as stated and the other team choosing the opposite. You can add your own topics in addition to the ones suggested.

Reporting History - Discuss several of the most important events in history and how these might have been reported in newspapers. Then, using the worksheet on page 46, have students choose an historic event and write about it in a newspaper article.

Web Sources

There are several useful sources of information on the Internet that you may wish to access during this unit. Most major newspapers have web sites where they include their most important stories and editorials. You should be able to find not only large metropolitan papers but also papers from other countries, small local papers, and specialty papers. You can access these sites using one of the following URLs. Since web sites change often, if these URLs are not available, you can access the newspapers by searching for "newspapers" in most search engines.

www.metaplus.com/pv/news/html
www.newspapers.com
www.interest.com/top100.html
www.thepaperboy.com
www.actualidad.com
www.newsdirectory.com
www.naa.org/hotlinks/index.asp
www.opinion-pages.org/

Another source that offers information on the history of newspapers is
www.encyclopedia.com/articles/09199.html

Vocabulary

Write a definition for each of these terms.

assigned news _____

_____

bias _____

_____

bold face _____

_____

byline _____

_____

caption _____

_____

censorship _____

_____

circulation _____

_____

dateline _____

_____

freedom of the press _____

_____

vocabulary, continued

headline _____

_____

edit _____

_____

editorial _____

_____

feature story _____

_____

journalism _____

_____

layout or make-up _____

_____

lead _____

_____

masthead _____

_____

news release _____

_____

Pulitzer Prize _____

_____

reporter _____

_____

syndicate _____

_____

History of Newspapers

People have always wanted to know what was happening in the world around them. When people lived in small groups, they could just spread news verbally from one person to another. When people started living in larger groups, they needed a more formalized way to let other people know what was happening. Newspapers developed as a way of distributing information on a regular basis.

The first known newspaper was produced by Julius Caesar's administration in 59 B.C. and called *Acta Diurna*. It was published daily and posted in public places. The Chinese also had a public newspaper, *pao* (meaning court circular), that was in circulation from 618 to 1911.

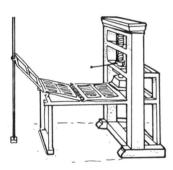

In the middle of the fifteenth century, Johann Gutenberg's invention of a printing press with moveable type marked a great change in printing technology and altered the way people could produce newspapers. It became easier to set the type for a newspaper, so new information could be issued more regularly. It also put printing in the hands of common people, so it was possible to distribute public newspapers without government control. By the early sixteenth century newspapers were being produced in Belgium, Italy, Germany, and The Netherlands. The year 1665 marked the beginning of the *London Gazette*, the first paper to be issued regularly in a newspaper format. The first newspaper in America (*Publick Occurences Both Foreign and Domestick* in 1690) was immediately banned by the British. The first regularly printed American newspaper was the *Boston Newsletter*, which originated in 1704.

The 1800s brought more changes to newspapers. In the beginning, newspapers were too expensive for ordinary people, so the only readers were the wealthy, educated elite. By the late 1800s, however, James Gordon and Horace Greeley began publishing penny papers, so more people could afford to buy newspapers. The late 1800s saw the beginning of "yellow journalism," sensational newspapers whose main goal was to attract readers, not necessarily to report accurate information. This name for vulgar, sensational journalism originated with the "Yellow Kid" comic strip that was published in Joseph Pulitzer's *New York World* newspaper.

Newspapers have enjoyed a long, influential role in the life and politics of nearly every nation in the world. In the late twentieth century, however,  radio, television and the Internet have taken away a lot of newspapers' business.

The News Story

5W + H

News articles are written to give people information. The goal is to reach as many readers as possible, so the information is presented in a very straightforward way so people can easily find the basic facts of the story. Each news story tries to answer the questions **who, what, where, when, why,** and **how** (5W + H). The answers to these questions are presented in a clear, well-organized, concise format.

Headline + Lead + Summary

The headline is a short statement that is written in large, bold type above the article. It draws people's attention to the article and gives them the basic facts of the story in as few words as possible.

The actual news article uses the "lead-and-summary" format. The first sentence and/or paragraph is the lead. It states the most important information. It does not answer all of the 5W + H questions, but it gives a brief statement of the story's basic facts or main theme.

The paragraphs that follow (the summary paragraphs) present additional information, summarize the main facts, or elaborate on the main theme. The additional facts are arranged in order of importance, with the most important facts at the beginning of the article.

Rules for Writing

News reporting follows certain rules. These rules are to ensure that the news is accurate and also that it is easy for readers to understand. News articles must be:

✓ **accurate** - Check your sources.
✓ **balanced** - Tell both sides of the story.
✓ **objective** - Be unbiased.
✓ **clear and concise** - Write to be understood.
✓ **recent** - Today's news is tomorrow's history.

Types of News Articles

As you read the newspaper, you will find several different types of news articles. Each type of article serves a different purpose and is written in a slightly different way.

Straight news stories report standard news in a conventional news reporting format. They are written to be informative and use the 5W + H format to report the most essential information in a well-organized format. Most current news is reported as straight news. After the initial story, the newspaper may follow up later with a feature story or an editorial.

The purpose of a **feature article** is to entertain or to supplement rather than to inform. It goes beyond the 5W + H format to give the reader a more in-depth perspective. A feature story is longer than a regular news article and is of interest to the general public. It can also include personal interviews and historical information. Feature stories often have an emotional, personal or humorous slant.

An **eyewitness story** is told by someone who was involved in the event. The reporter gives details of the event and also describes what he or she saw and felt. The story must be factual, but the writer may interject a personal perspective.

An **investigative news story** is an in-depth report that presents information that has a significant bearing on public affairs. It is usually based on information that is not public and the reporter must be somewhat of a detective to get the information. It often uncovers wrongdoing.

Special Projects

1. Find a news story that is of interest to you. Decide what kind of article it is. Then write a summary of the article.

2. Assume that you are a reporter who is writing a feature article. Choose a topic and/or a person you will interview. Make a list of ten good questions you could ask.

3. Write a feature or a straight news story about something or someone in your school or a group to which you belong.

Eyewitness News Story

An eyewitness news article offers a more personal viewpoint than other types of news stories. In these stories, the writer tells how it felt to be involved in the event. He or she reports the facts but also gives his or her personal impressions. Look around you and you'll see potential news stories. Write an eyewitness news article about one of the following events, giving details that describe what was happening as you experienced the event.

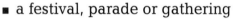

- A newsworthy weather phenomenon (hurricane, earthquake, serious storm, heat wave)
- a festival, parade or gathering
- a sports event
- some other activity in which you have been involved

_____

_____

_____

_____

_____

_____

_____

_____

_____

_____

_____

_____

_____

_____

_____

_____

_____

_____

(Continue on another piece of paper.)

News Photography

1 Picture = 1,000 Words

An important part of any newspaper is the photographs that accompany the news articles. They draw people's attention to the stories and show visually what happened. Photographers must be skilled at getting pictures that will add to or illustrate the content of the news report. A news photographer who is assigned to spot news must be ready to move fast to get pictures of the news as it is happening. Assigned news photographers know about an event in advance. They can plan the pictures and get them exactly the way they want them.

Find photographs in your local newspaper that are examples of spot and assigned news photographs. Paste them in the space below and/or on the back of this paper.

Special Projects

1. Be a photographer for your school, club or community. Take black and white photographs of an event and write a news release to accompany the photos.

2. Read the newspaper for a week and select the best photographs. Tell why you think they are exceptional.

Parts of a Newspaper

A newspaper is a daily or weekly publication that distributes news, usually domestic, local and foreign. In addition to reporting various news happenings, it can include in-depth reports, forecasts, humor, and advice. Newspapers are usually divided into sections, with each section specializing in a particular type of news. You can find sections of a newspaper devoted to sports, business, local news, national news, world news, entertainment, comics, home and garden, editorial, classified advertisements, and more. Each section will run news and have feature articles that relate to that topic.

In which of these sections of the newspaper would you find the following headlines?

local	state	national	world
business	entertainment	sports	home and garden

_____   *Oil Prices Soar Worldwide*

_____   *City Bus Service Stalled*

_____   *Is Peace in the Middle East Possible?*

_____   *Star Quarterback Sidelined with Injuries*

_____   *Forest Fire Threatens State Park*

_____   *Local Bank Robbed for the Fourth Time*

_____   *Quilt and Hobby Show Draws Record Crowds*

_____   *World Leaders Meet to Discuss Disarmament*

_____   *Local Girl Wins State Spelling Bee*

_____   *Local High School Team Advances to State Playoffs*

_____   *Stock Market Up for Fifth Straight Week*

_____   *A Natural Cure for Snails*

_____   *Festival Seeks Volunteers*

Special Project

Find headlines from your local newspaper for each section of the newspaper. On a separate piece of paper, write the section of the paper and a headline.

News Coverage

A column inch is the way newspapers measure how much space is allotted to a particular article, photo or advertisement. An article that spans 3 columns and is 5 inches deep would be 15 column inches (3 x 5 = 15), while an article that occupies one column but is 12 inches long is 12 column inches (1 x 12 = 12).

B.3   LOCAL/STATE

Mistaken Identity
Couple drive off in wrong car
WRONG KEY
STARTS WRONG
VEHICLE

Find out how your newspaper allocates space for different kinds of news. Survey the first three pages of the paper for one week. Keep track of the amount of space devoted to each category of news. Then find the average for the week.

	day 1	day 2	day 3	day 4	day 5	day 6	day 7	average
world news	___	___	___	___	___	___	___	___
national news	___	___	___	___	___	___	___	___
local news	___	___	___	___	___	___	___	___
human interest	___	___	___	___	___	___	___	___
SPORTS	___	___	___	___	___	___	___	___
other	___	___	___	___	___	___	___	___

Compare your results with those of classmates who surveyed different papers. What generalizations can you make about your newspaper?

_____

_____

_____

_____

Local News

Local issues are often found on the front page, but you may find local news throughout the newspaper. You also find local issues reported in a special local section of the newspaper. This section deals with events in your community or surrounding communities. This is where you may find information about local happenings or decisions by regional officials, announcements of upcoming meetings, requests for volunteers, birth announcements, obituaries, weddings and social events.

Choose an event that has happened in your community. Write an article about this event. Remember to include:

- ✓ who was involved
- ✓ what happened
- ✓ when it happened
- ✓ where it happened
- ✓ why it happened
- ✓ how it happened

_____

_____

_____

_____

_____

_____

_____

_____

_____

_____

_____

_____

_____

_____

(Continue on another piece of paper.)

World and National News

Things that happen in other parts of the nation or in other countries of the world affect what is happening in your location. A labor dispute in one country can cause an increase in the cost of products in other countries. A drought in one area affects the availability of food products from that region. When oil-producing countries decide to raise the price of crude oil, automobile owners and truckers around the world feel the pinch. For this reason, people need to know what is happening beyond the boundaries of their own community.

Metropolitan newspapers offer a lot of information about what is happening in the other parts of the nation and the world. Local newspaper carry some national and world news, but it is usually more abbreviated coverage. You usually find world news on the front page but it can also appear in a special section for world news.

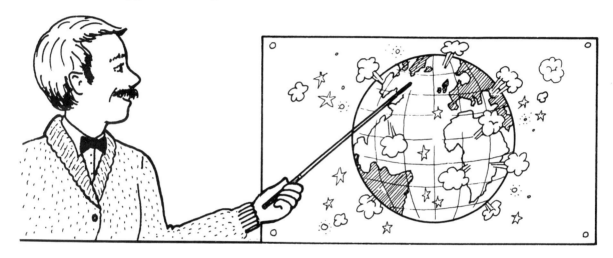

Choose two world or national news stories and briefly tell what the article is about by answering who, what, where, when, why and how.

	Story 1	Story 2
who?	_____	_____
what?	_____	_____
	_____	_____
where?	_____	_____
when?	_____	_____
why?	_____	_____
	_____	_____
how?	_____	_____
	_____	_____

News Services

Have you ever wondered where all the news stories come from? Many of the articles about happenings in other places in the world are written by people who are employed by a news service (like the Associated Press or United Press International) or are written by people who work for newspapers in other cities. Press services send reporters to other countries and then provide subscribing newspapers with news reports, photographs, and special columns. This makes it possible for local newspaper publishers to provide information about news around the world without having to send reporters there. These services have been around since the 1930s.

Find out when a newspaper publisher would use a news service (like AP or UPI), another newspaper, or press releases. Find examples of articles from each source. Make a listing of a couple of articles from each source.

news service	*other papers*	*news release*
_____	_____	_____
_____	_____	_____
_____	_____	_____
_____	_____	_____

Combine your information with other people in your class. Based on this survey of articles, when does your newspaper use articles from a news service?_____

_____

When does it use articles from press releases? _____

_____

When does it use articles from other papers?_____

_____

Opinion Page

The editorial page of the newspaper contains the views or opinions of the editor and editorial columnists. It is sometimes called the "opinion page." The article that is called the "editorial" voices the opinion of the publisher or the editor and is most often based on something that is happening in the news. Newspapers have different political stances that will be reflected in these articles. Some are very conservative and some are very liberal. While reading this section of the paper, readers need to remember that while these articles include facts, they are not unbiased.

The editorial page will have an editorial cartoon that expresses an opinion or visually depicts an event in the news. This section will usually also contain a section for reader comments (letters to the editor). This is where readers can write in to agree or disagree with things that the editor or the columnists have said or can comment on things that are happening in their community or in the world.

Choose one article from the editorial page. State the issue and the opinion of the person writing the article.

Article title _____

Issue _____

_____

Position _____

_____

_____

Do you agree? Why or why not? _____

_____

_____

Letters to the Editor

Letters to the editor can be positive (praising someone or something that has happened), negative (offering criticism), or merely pointing out a situation that needs attention. When you write a letter to the editor you first must be clear about what your objective is. Your letter should clearly state your position and then back it up with logical reasons or verifiable facts.

Read five letters to the editor and identify why the person was writing and what his or her feelings were. Then respond to one of these letters. Write your letter to the editor, giving your reasons for agreeing or disagreeing with the person who wrote the original letter.

_____ ,

Political Cartoons

Everyone is familiar with the cartoons in the comic section of the newspaper, but some cartoons in a newspaper are not found in the comic section. Political or satirical cartoons are usually found on the editorial pages. These cartoons poke fun at events or people who are in the news or show a news event in a pictorial way. They are designed to express an opinion.

1. Find several examples of this type of cartoon and attach them to this paper.

2. Why are political cartoons found on the editorial page and not in the comics section?

_____

_____

3. Compare the similarities and differences between a daily comic strip and a political cartoon.

How are they alike? _____

_____

How are they different? _____

_____

Which has the most impact? _____

_____

Special Projects

1. Make a collection of political cartoons for a two-week period. Categorize them according to subject matter or political message.

2. Create an editorial cartoon that shows a real-life situation in your community.

Humor in the Newspaper

You naturally think of newspapers as a source of serious news, but did you realize that humor is a part of many newspapers? This humor can take many forms. Besides the comics, humor can be found in editorial cartoons, stories about humorous events, funny essays by columnists, and whimsical photographs. These comical additions to the serious side of newspapers are designed to make them more attractive to a wide variety of readers.

Collect examples of three different kinds of humor in your newspaper. Attach them to this paper and label them. Below tell whether they are cartoons, articles or photographs and explain why each one is humorous.

Example 1 is a _____ about_____

It is funny because _____

_____

_____

Example 2 is a _____ about_____

It is funny because _____

_____

_____

Example 3 is a _____ about_____

It is funny because _____

_____

_____

Special Project

Write a humorous story for a newspaper based on something that has happened to you.

The Comics

A comic strip is a sequence of drawings that tells a funny incident or an adventure. A cartoonist will develop a set of characters and use these characters in the humorous incidents. While many cartoons are comical, comic strips also involve science fiction, adventure, and crime fighting. Cartoons have been a part of daily newspapers for a long time. While papers began using cartoons in the eighteenth century, comic strips were first used during the twentieth century to attract readers to the newspapers.

1. Read all the comic strips for one week.

2. Which comics do you think are the best? _____

_____

3. Which comics do you think are the least interesting? _____

_____

4. What would you like to say to the creator of one of these strips? _____

_____

_____

DANDY TOONS

Special Project

Create a cartoon strip that shows something funny that could happen in your school or home.

Business News

Are you interested in making more money? Want to find out how to manage the money you do have? Do you need to check the current prices of the stocks you own? Then open your newspaper to the business section. The business section of the newspaper contains important news about local, national or world-wide companies. It may include articles about how to better run your business if you are a business owner, as well as articles about how to manage your money, how to be a better consumer, and notices about upcoming business-related events. This section also includes information about the stock market.

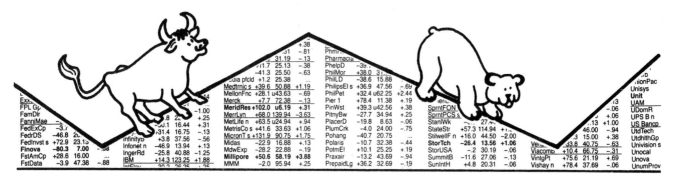

1. Look through the business section. Find some information that you think would be useful either in your future job, in investing, or in running a business.

Name of article _____

Useful information _____

_____

2. Identify the most active stocks. What general area(s) of business do they represent?

stock   type of business

_____   _____

_____   _____

_____   _____

_____   _____

Special Project

1. Select two stocks and follow their prices for two weeks. Make a graph of their prices each day.

2. Find a summary of a business story on the Internet or find out what is happening with a business in your community. Collect additional information. Use this information to write a news article that would be interesting to people your age.

Sports

Almost every newspaper has a sports section. In this section you will find information about the outcomes of sporting events, profiles of players, and articles about issues in sports like player's salaries, the behavior of fans, endorsements, sports-related injuries or the role of referees. In this section you can also find statistics about teams and individual players as well as team standings. You will find not only information about local sporting events but also college and professional sporting events for nearly every sport. If you want to know what has happened or what is going to happen in sports, this is the section of the newspaper to read.

1. What unique words are used in sports headlines? Make a list of some of the most attention-getting headlines.

_____

_____

_____

_____

(Continue on the back of this paper.)

2. Use this list to make a list of words and phrases that are synonyms for "win" and "lose."

win

_____
_____
_____
_____
_____
_____

lose

_____
_____
_____
_____
_____
_____

Special Project

1. Choose your favorite sport and make a collage of this sport using pictures and words from the newspaper. Design it to communicate an idea or feeling.

2. Write an eyewitness account of a sports event you recently attended.

Humorous Sports

A fan leans over the wall to catch a fly ball and falls onto the playing field. A basketball player gets confused and makes a shot in the opponent's basket. A football player catches the ball and runs in the wrong direction. Sometimes articles in the sports section will report humorous things that happen to players and fans. These articles add additional interest to one of the most popular sections of the newspaper.

1. Find at least two humorous sports articles. Write the headlines for the articles.

   Humorous Headline 1 - _____

   Humorous Headline 2 - _____

2. Write your own newspaper article about a humorous thing that happened (or could happen) while you were playing your favorite sport.

   _____

_____
_____
_____
_____
_____
_____
_____
_____
_____
_____
_____
_____
_____
_____
_____
_____

    © Dandy Lion Publications - *In the News*

Entertainment

Want to know what movies are playing? Are you planning to attend a concert by the latest, greatest music group? Want to know if that new play is worth seeing or if the movie playing down the street is appropriate for your young cousin? Whether you're planning a night of television watching or looking for a good art gallery showing, you can find the information you need in the newspaper in a section that typically has a name like "entertainment," "date book," "movies," or "community and arts." It may even be a separate section of the paper. In this section you will find information about every kind of leisure activity you could ever want to experience.

What kinds of information can you find in this section of the newspaper?

_____

_____

_____

_____

_____

Special Projects

1. Choose a book that you have read that you think would make a good movie. Create an advertisement for a movie that could be made from the book. Include all the information that you found while looking at other movie advertisements in the newspaper.

2. Analyze the rating of movies currently advertised in the movie section of your newspaper. Create a chart that shows how many movies are appropriate for each age group or that receive a particular rating.

3. Based on these figures, what recommendations would you make to the people who produce movies? Write a letter to the Film Makers Guild to explain your feelings and the reasons why you feel this way.

Travel Information

Where do you want to go for vacation? Whether you want to take an exotic cruise or check out the hiking trails in a national park, you'll find the information in the newspaper. Most newspapers have a special weekly section devoted to travel news. Here you will find articles about travel destinations, information about how to be a savvy traveler, and tips about special prices.

Read several travel articles. Notice the vivid language the writer uses. Then write a travel article about some place you have visited recently. Include a picture.

_____

(headline)

_____
_____
_____
_____
_____
_____
_____
_____
_____
_____
_____
_____
_____
_____
_____
_____

(Continue on another piece of paper.)

Weather

Should you take an umbrella today? Is it going to be windy enough to fly a kite? What's the weather like in the city where you will spend your vacation? Luckily all sorts of information about the weather (past, present and future) can be found in the weather section of the newspaper. Not only can you find forecasts for your community, but you will often be able to get temperatures for cities in other parts of the world.

Look at the weather section of your newspaper and find the latest weather statistics for your community.

high temperature _____

normal/average high _____

low temperature _____

normal/average low _____

precipitation _____

sunrise _____

sunset _____

What weather is forecast for the next couple of days?

_____

_____

What symbols are used for these weather conditions?

sun	rain	clouds	snow or ice

Special Project

Make a chart that shows at least two different weather statistics (like high and low temperatures) for your community for a week.

Advertising

It costs a lot of money to pay for reporters, photographers, office people, computers, printing presses and paper to produce a newspaper. Advertising pays for much of the cost of producing newspapers. For newspapers that charge a subscription fee, the production costs are paid for by both the subscriptions, the over-the-counter sales and advertising. The cost of producing free newspapers is paid entirely by the advertising. In most newspapers, advertisements take up 60% of the space, and news and commentary account for 40%. Advertisements are measured in column inches, and the charge for advertising is based on the rate times the number of column inches.

Take a survey to find out how much of the newspaper (not including the classified advertising section) is devoted to advertising. Categorize the advertising in a daily and a Sunday newspaper according to products (cars, homes, food, clothing, etc.).

product categories	daily paper	Sunday paper

Special Project

Show your findings in a graph or chart on another piece of paper.

Classified Advertisements

The classified advertisements section is a special part of the newspaper that is somewhat different from ads in the other sections. Sometimes this section is called the "want ads." Classified ads are brief advertisements, typically one column wide, that offer or request specific items like jobs, pets, household goods, houses, apartments, or cars. Each type of ad is in a special section so people can easily find the items that they are looking for.

1. Study the classified advertising section to see what kind of advertisements catch your attention. Then write a want ad for one of these categories.
   - real estate
   - pets
   - automobile
   - office equipment

2. Use the information in the classified section to figure out how much it would cost to place your ad in the newspaper for one week.

   cost = _____

WANTED

_____

_____

_____

_____

_____

_____

_____

_____

_____

_____

Special Projects

1. Read the help wanted or job opportunity ads in the classified section of the newspaper. List several jobs that you find interesting. What special training, education, or skills would you need for this job? Write a letter expressing your interest and stating your qualifications.

2. Read several job opportunity advertisements and note the kind of information that is usually included in the ads. Then write a help wanted advertisement for a job that could exist in the future that does not exist now.

Using Newspaper Advertising

You are planning an outing for your class and are in charge of the food. Plan a menu and then use the advertisements for food to make a shopping list and calculate the total cost.

Menu

_____

_____

_____

_____

_____

_____

_____

_____

_____

items to buy	quantity	price	place to buy

Newspaper People

Through the ages, many people have contributed to the development of the modern newspaper. Match each of these people with the phrase or words that describe his contribution.

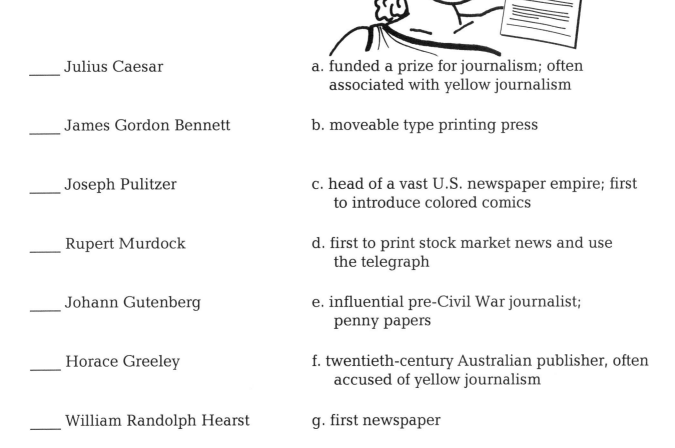

____ Julius Caesar

____ James Gordon Bennett

____ Joseph Pulitzer

____ Rupert Murdock

____ Johann Gutenberg

____ Horace Greeley

____ William Randolph Hearst

a. funded a prize for journalism; often associated with yellow journalism

b. moveable type printing press

c. head of a vast U.S. newspaper empire; first to introduce colored comics

d. first to print stock market news and use the telegraph

e. influential pre-Civil War journalist; penny papers

f. twentieth-century Australian publisher, often accused of yellow journalism

g. first newspaper

Special Projects

1. Choose one of these men or some other notable journalist, publisher, or photo journalist. Write a report outlining his or her contributions.

2. Find out what the Pulitzer Prize is and in what areas of journalism it is given. Make a list of the criteria you would use if you were the judge for this prize. Design the award that you would give the winners.

News in the Future

When newspapers began, they were the most efficient way of getting current news to a large number of people. As new forms of media have developed, their popularity has changed. Radio, television and the Internet have eaten away at newspaper readership. Many newspapers have gone out of business or combined with competing papers as their readers switch to alternative ways of getting the news.

Assuming that in the future, newspapers will be replaced by electronic news services, write an epitaph for the last newspaper.

_____

_____

_____

_____

_____

_____

_____

_____

_____

_____

_____

_____

_____

Special Project

Discuss (verbally or in writing) the advantages and disadvantages of newspapers versus electronic news.

Debatable Topics

Newspapers have been an important element in social and political life for hundreds of years. A free press keeps citizens informed and allows for an exchange of ideas and information. There are, however, many criticisms of newspapers.

Form debate teams to debate one of the following issues. Have one side take the position as it is stated and the other side take the opposing position.

Resolved: Reporters should have the right to withhold confidential sources of information.

Resolved: Newspapers should have complete freedom of speech.

Resolved: Newspapers should only accept advertisements that are fair and truthful.

Resolved: Because newspapers are important for the functioning of our political system and economy, they should be subsidized by the government.

Resolved: Newspapers should be replaced by electronic media.

A Great Moment

THE MAIN STREET JOURNAL

Newspaper reporters are always right on the spot, ready to get all the facts of an event so they can report it to their readers. They have recorded the greatest events in history on their front pages. They have investigated and exposed scandals, uncovered wrongdoing, and recognized charitable actions.

How would some of the greatest moments in history be reported in a newspaper? Choose a favorite historical event and find as many facts about the event as possible. Create a headline and news article to report the incident. Indicate in which section of the newspaper this article would appear.

_____

_____

_____

_____

_____

_____

_____

_____

_____

_____

_____

_____

_____

_____

_____

_____

_____

_____

(Continue on another piece of paper.)

Answers

What is a Newspaper? - pg. 24
Oil Prices - world
City Bus - local
Peace in Middle East - world
Star Quarterback - sports
Forest Fire - state
Bank Robbed - local
Hobby Show - local/home and garden
World Leaders - world
Spelling Bee - local
State Playoffs - sports
Stock Market - national
Snail Cure - home and garden
Festival Volunteers - local

Newspaper People - pg. 43
Caesar - g
Bennett - d
Pulitzer - a
Murdock - f
Gutenberg - b
Greeley - e
Hearst - c